OVERTHINKING
TURN OFF YOUR THOUGHTS

How to Overcome Your Destructive Thoughts and Start Thinking Positively
Beginner's Guide: How To Stop Procrastination

Table of Contents

INTRODUCTION

How many times have you stayed up late at night because you cannot stop worrying about that one little slip-up you had at work? Now, how many times have you lost yourself in your thoughts for long stretches of time about that one embarrassing thing that you did back when you were in high school? This is just the tip of the iceberg when you are suffering from chronic overthinking.

You might seem a bit confused about what could be wrong about thinking too much? Is it not good? Getting lost in your thoughts is relatively harmless, but that is not what overthinking is. Overthinking is when your mind gets overloaded by a couple of negative thoughts that seem to be on an endless loop, that keeps playing faster and faster. When you do manage to stop overthinking, you will notice that you have already wasted a lot of time, and that you are also mentally and physically drained of energy.

This book aims to help you identify the reasons why you are constantly overthinking, and you will also learn a couple of tips and techniques on how you can pull yourself out of the death spiral of overthinking before you can fall in any deeper.

Just a disclaimer though, it is still best for you to get professional help if you feel that your mental health has been greatly compromised. This book is just a guide to help you prevent your overthinking from getting any worse, and maybe minimize its effects, but to get rid of it permanently, it is best that you get help from professional psychiatrists. However, if your overthinking problem is not that serious, you can use the tips in this book to make your symptoms more manageable.

CHAPTER 1

HOW TO STOP OVERTHINKING

Overthinking is one of the most common mental conditions in the world, and unfortunately, it is also one of the most debilitating. You might think that it is no big deal, everybody gets lost in their thoughts sometimes, right? But when overthinking hits you, it hits you hard. This is especially troubling if you have trouble with anxiety.

Now, if you have any previous experience in falling into the almost endless spiraling pit of despair that is overthinking, then you know just how horrible it is. Overthinking can prevent you from enjoying the things that you used to love doing, like going to parties, walking in the park, or just meeting with friends. Overthinking can also negatively affect your performance at work, it makes you lose motivation, makes you procrastinate on your tasks, and thus ruining whatever chances of job progression you might have. Overthinking can also ruin your personal relationships; no one wants to be around a person who is always complaining, cranky, and has such a short temper, so you will have very few friends, and they might not be sticking around for much longer.

If the picture painted above seems familiar to you, then you are probably already aware that there is something wrong about you, and that you are already desperate to find a way to fix yourself and start living again. However, it seems like everything you do seems futile, it's as if there is always an insurmountable hurdle in front of you. Overthinking not only leaves you mentally drained, it also makes you feel exhausted physically. It's like having an energy vampire latched permanently on your neck, and it is constantly feeding on what little mental and physical energy you have.

However, you should not lose hope just yet, there are plenty of ways that you can use to overcome your chronic overthinking problem. But first, you need to start with understanding the core problem; you need to know what overthinking is, and from there you can start looking for the most viable solutions.

Overthinking Disorder Defined

Everyone gets sucked into the rabbit hole of obsessive thoughts sometimes, and when it happens occasionally then it is fine. However, when overthinking starts to consume your life that is when it becomes a chronic mental problem.

Not everyone is prone to overthinking, but some are more likely to suffer from it. For instance, people with a history of struggling with anxiety are almost always dealing with overthinking and its consequences on a daily basis. In fact, overthinking is actually one of the triggers that cause anxiety in most people.

Even if you do not have any history of mental health problems, if you consider yourself as a "problem solver" of sorts, then you are prone to overthinking. The thing you consider as your most valuable asset, which is your analytical mind, can become your worst enemy when your overthinking is triggered. Analytical thinkers are the ones that are easily pulled into an endless loop of unproductive and irrational thoughts.

In addition, if you are at a low point in your life where you have unusually high levels of uncertainty, it can trigger your overthinking disorder. If you just experienced a major loss in your life, like you just got fired from your job, your significant other left you, or someone close to you recently died, these events might cause your mind to uncontrollably spiral of unproductive thoughts.

What are the Symptoms of Overthinking?

Now that you have an idea of what overthinking is, the next thing that you need to know is the signs of overthinking to look out for. Knowing the symptoms will inform you that you might need to be wary of the status of your mental health, maybe consider getting professional help. You can somehow gauge how deep into overthinking you are by identifying which symptoms have already manifested; if you find that you have signs of being a chronic overthinker, then you should probably consider getting professional help ASAP.

You Have Trouble Getting to Sleep

You cannot turn off your thoughts, even when you try; in fact, your thoughts actually start racing even faster when you try to stop them. All of these worries and doubts swirling in your head agitates you and prevents you from getting enough rest.

Overthinkers know the feeling of not getting enough sleep, almost too well actually. Insomnia happens because you have no control over your brain, you cannot shut off the chain of negative thoughts going through your mind at a hundred miles an hour. All of the things that worried you throughout the day comes back just when you hit the sack, and you feel so wired that you cannot fall asleep.

If you are having difficulty calming your mind on your own, you can try different relaxing activities before you go to bed. There are plenty of things that might help you ease your mind just enough to let you get some sleep, like meditation, writing on a journal, adult coloring books, drawing, painting, reading a book, or even just having a nice conversation with a loved one. Do anything that can shift your attention away from the negative thoughts long enough for you to get some sleep.

You Start to Self-Medicate

Numerous medical researches have discovered that most people suffering from overthinking disorder have turned to using recreational drugs, alcohol, overeating, or other ways to somehow get a grip on their emotions. Overthinkers feel the need to rely on external stimuli because they believe that their internal resources (aka their minds) are already compromised.

It is never a good idea to turn to try to treat yourself from overthinking. Odds are, you will still be overthinking afterwards, and you have to deal with a different problem brought about by your self-medication.

You are Always Tired

If you are constantly feeling tired, you need to take action. Fatigue is your body's way of telling you to listen to it because there is something wrong going on; you should not ignore it and just hop from one activity to the next.

Usually, fatigue is caused by physical overexertion and lack of rest. However, overthinking can also cause fatigue and exhaustion. Your mind is like a muscle; if you are constantly burdening it with dozens of heavy, negative thoughts all the time, and not even giving it some time to recover, it will get exhausted and cause you to burn out.

Back when humans were still living off the land, people did not have that many things to worry about, which means they do not have quite as many things to think about as well. In today's modern world, people lead complicated lives that require them to accomplish a lot of things in a short amount of time. In this fast-paced world, the need to slow down every once in a while is crucial for people's well-being. So, whenever you feel fatigued, or better yet, if you feel close to it, slow things down and figure out what your body, and your mind, needs before doing anything else.

You Tend to Overanalyze Everything

Overthinkers have one major problem, and that is that they always feel that they need to be in control of everything. They plan out every aspect of their lives, some of them even go as far as planning up to the smallest detail. They feel that doing this is the only way they can feel safe, but it always seem to backfire at them because it is actually impossible to plan for everything that will happen in their lives.

Even so, they still continue to plan out their futures, and they get anxious when unexpected things happen; and there always seem to be unexpected things happening all the time. Overthinkers hate dealing with things that they do not have control over, they fear the unknown. When unexpected problems do surface, they cause them to sit and mull things over instead of taking immediate action to solve the unexpected problem. Numerous medical studies have shown that overthinking leads to making poor judgment calls, which is why overthinking does not really help.

When you catch yourself just before you start overthinking, try your best to bring your thoughts back to the present by taking deep breaths and thinking happy thoughts. Before your negative thoughts go rampant inside your head, acknowledge them, and think about what they can do for you presently; doing this alone is usually enough to get rid of these negative thoughts, because you will discover that their only purpose is to cause you stress.

You are Afraid of Failure

You fancy yourself a perfectionist, and you often think about how awful you would feel if you were to somehow fail. This fear of failure can be so strong that it paralyzes you, and it keeps you from learning from your prior mistakes, which often lead to you repeating them.

Overthinkers often cannot accept failure, and they will do everything they can to avoid it. Ironically, they think that the only way to not fail is to do nothing at all. They mistakenly believe that in order to avoid failure, they should not put themselves in a position to fail at all, which also means they are not in the position to succeed as well.

If this sounds like you, remember that you are more than just your failures; no one could even remember the last time that you screwed up, it's just you. Also, keep in mind that it is impossible to escape failure, and you should never avoid it at all. For failure allows you to grow and evolve.

You are Afraid of What the Future Holds

Instead of being excited of the things that you are yet to experience, your anxiety and fear of what could go wrong paralyzes you into doing nothing.

If you are afraid of what the future could bring, then your fear keeps you trapped inside your own mind. Research shows that this fear of the future can be so crippling that sufferers tend to turn to drugs and/or alcohol just so they can tune out the negative thoughts that are clamoring inside their heads.

You Don't Trust Your Own Judgment

You cannot help yourself from second-guessing all of your decisions; from your outfit, what you will be having for lunch, or even what you will be doing for the day. You are always afraid that you will be making the wrong choices, and you often rely on others to reassure you that you made the right call.

Overthinkers, as mentioned earlier, are natural perfectionists; they constantly analyze, re-analyze, and re-analyze again, all situations that they find themselves in. They do not want to put themselves in a position where there is even a slight chance of failure. They do not want to make the wrong choice, so they take their sweet time making up their mind; they do not trust themselves enough to make the right decision for anything. They are so out of touch from their intuition that all of their decisions come from their brain, and this is not always right as there are times when you just need to follow your gut instinct. In addition, if your brain is bogged down from dozens of negative thoughts, it is hard to make a clear decision.

You Suffer from Frequent Tension Headaches

Tension headaches feel as if there is a thick rubber band wrapped around your temples, and it is slowly getting tighter. Aside from headache, you might also feel a sharp pain or stiffness in your neck. If you suffer from chronic tension headaches, it is a sign that you are overworking yourself and you need a rest.

And by rest, it also includes rest from mental activities, like overthinking. Headaches is a sign that your body needs to take a break, this includes your mind. In addition, you might not notice it, but when you overthink, you are actually thinking of the same things over and over again.

Overthinkers usually have negative thought patterns that loop around themselves. To fight this, you need to break this loop by reinforcing positive thoughts. Take deep breaths, and focus your mind on every time your chest rises and falls, being mindful of the present will help you get rid of negative thoughts and the tension headache that came with them.

Stiff Joints and Muscle Pain

It might sound far fetched, but overthinking can actually affect your entire body, not just your mind. And once your physical body is affected by your out of control negative thoughts, it will not be long until your emotional well-being gets hit too. Until you address and get rid of the underlying issues that cause you to overthink, the body pains will continue. Overthinking might start in your mind, but its effects will gradually creep into the other parts of your body.

You Cannot Stay In the Present

When you overthink, you will find it difficult living in the present moment and actually enjoy your life as it happens. Overthinking causes you to lose focus on the things happening around you, you are so engrossed at thinking about your problems over and over that it seems like you are trapped inside your own mind. If your mind gets bogged down by a ton of unnecessary thoughts, you are removing yourself from the present, and this can and will negatively affect your personal relationships.

You need to open yourself to the world around you, do not let yourself get too wrapped up in negative thoughts. The only thoughts that you should allow inside your mind are those that serve your well-being; ignore and forget about the ones that bring you down. There are so much beauty in life, and the opportunities for incredible experiences are unlimited, however, you can only appreciate them if you can manage to tune out the idle chatter in your mind and start listening to your heart instead.

Different Causes of Overthinking

Again, there is nothing wrong about thinking about your problems so you can think of a solution for them, it becomes worrisome when you have a bad habit of twisting narratives around in your head until you can see every angle and side to it. Overthinking is not productive as it just makes you dwell over your problems; you are not looking for a solution for them, and you are only making yourself feel miserable.

In order to find an effective way to break your overthinking habit, you need to find out what caused it in the first place. Below are some of the more common reasons as to why people tend to overthink their problems rather than actually find a solution for them.

1. Lack of Self-confidence

If you are not self-confident, you tend to doubt every little thing that you say or do. When you hesitate, even a little, about the things that you want to do, you are letting uncertainty and fear creep into your mind, and it will be very difficult to get them out of there. You can never really tell what your decisions will take you; even if you planned every little detail, the outcome will still not be exactly what you hoped for (it could either be better or worse than what you planned). This is why you should learn to take risks and not torture yourself when you did not get the results you wished for.

2. When You Worry Too Much

It is only natural to worry when you encounter new and unfamiliar things and events. However, if you worry too much that you cannot even imagine a positive outcome, then it will trigger you to overthink. This is problematic because worry attracts even more problems, sometimes it creates ones out of thin air, which cause overthinking to go even deeper. Instead of mulling over how things could go wrong, it is better to entertain thoughts that are more positive, like how much better you would feel if a certain even turns in your favor.

3. When You Overthink to Protect Yourself

Some people believe that they can protect themselves from troubles whenever they overthink, but the truth is that overthinking is a trap that kills your progress. Overthinking and not doing anything to change the status quo might seem good, but stifling your progress is never a good thing at all. In addition, when you overthink, you are not really staying at the same position, you are actually undoing whatever amount of progress you achieved thus far.

4. You are Unable to "Turn Off" Your Mind

Many overthinkers became that way because they cannot seem to get their minds off their problems no matter how hard they try. People who are sensitive to stress live as if they are constantly wound up tightly, they have somehow forgotten how to relax and change their chain of thoughts. Overthinking happens when a person stresses too much on a single problem, and he could not turn his focus away from it.

5. You are Always Chasing After Perfection

Being a perfectionist is not necessarily a good thing. In fact, one could argue that being a perfectionist is not good at all. Most people who struggle with perfectionism are constantly anxious. They often wake up in the middle of the night thinking of the things that they could have done better. Being a perfectionist causes overthinking because you are always trying to outdo yourself.

6. Overthinking is Your Habit

Overthinking is not always caused by a person's bad habits, sometimes overthinking IS the person's bad habit. For some people, it does not take much for them to overthink; they usually default to overthinking the moment that they encounter even minor inconvenience. This bad habit prevents people from living their lives the way they actually wanted to.

7. Reliance on Quick Fixes

With the advent of the internet also came a myriad of self-help videos, articles, and websites. The one thing that these resources promise is that they can help fix what ails you in a couple of of easy steps. Of course, all of them are lying, but unfortunately, people usually have no other choice. However, there are many quick fixes that really do help, and that is the reason why it is problematic.

Are you hungry? Just order a pizza or Chinese takeout using your phone. You do not like walking? Get yourself a car. Do you need to talk to your mother halfway across the country? Pick up your smartphone and start a video call. The modern world has so many quick fixes in place for almost every kind of problem that people might have. However, quick fixes just work most of the time, not every time. When a person's problem remains unresolved for a few hours, or even days, his mind automatically defaults to thinking that there must be something wrong, and this usually triggers overthinking.

For instance, if you are feeling blue or upset for a couple of days, there must be some kind of quick fix for it right? You think you need to quit your job, break up with your SO, stop talking to your parents; yes, these things might provide some form of cure for what ails you, but are these the correct choices, not necessarily. These options are band-aid fixes, not really long-term solutions. And when these band-aid fixes eventually fail, people immediately fall into the spiral of overthinking.

8. Modern Life is Full of Chronic Stressors

When you feel stressed, the explanations that come to your mind are not the complete story. There are literally dozens of factors that might have contributed to your negative emotions, the things that you thought might be the reasons are just the tip of the iceberg.

For instance, when you feel lethargic, you might think that it must be because you are unhappy with your job, or if you are having problems with your family, it does not even scrape your mind that you need more sleep because you are just skipping one hour of sleep. However, lack of sleep actually stacks up, and if you skip an hour of sleep every day for a week, your body will reflect all of the stresses that you have accumulated.

It is like the myth of the frog placed in a pot of cold water that is gradually brought to a boil; the change in temperature is so gradual that the frog does not even try to jump out of the pot, and stays there until it is boiled alive.

9. Dreaming Has a Cost

Western culture respects, and actually encourages people to pursue their dreams. This is not really a problem, it can be a positive actually, but when people believe that they can achieve their dreams with little to no effort that is when things go bad. Most children grow up believing that they just need to be good little boys and girls to get ahead in life, but then when they reach adulthood, the magic vanishes.

When a person first experiences the less than stellar world of the 9 to 5 office desk job, real relationship problems, and how incredibly bland and normal real life is, they start to think of all the things that they might have done wrong for them to deserve their vanilla lives. When the gap between fantasy and reality becomes too great, it causes great sadness, which also cause them to give up on chasing their dreams.

Many people are conditioned to believing that they are entitled to achieving their dreams, and when they do not get what they wanted, they start overthinking. Again, it is not inherently bad to dream, just do not expect them to come true just because you wished them they would. This feeling of entitlement often leads to overthinking.

For example, one person might think that there must be something wrong with the system because he did not get that promotion he worked hard to get, or why he is not feeling the effects of the economic boom that has been reported all over the news lately? This leads to even darker thoughts like maybe the reason he did not get that promotion was because he did not graduate from an Ivy League university. He starts blaming his parents for not paying for an Ivy League education. He also starts thinking that maybe it is his family that is holding him back from success, or maybe the system at his work is rigged for him to fail. Or maybe, it is just that he is not as smart or as capable as his co-workers. All of these thoughts will start swirling around the person's head.

10. Introspection Went Too Far

Although emotional awareness is still important, but you need to find the happy medium for it to become beneficial. The truth is that most men have ignored emotional awareness altogether, while most women have take it a bit too far. This resulted in many women sitting and talking about their emotions, but rather than actually trying to fix their problems, this turns into an act where they are just finding validation for their emotions. Not only is this kind of thing not helpful to your plight, it can also be harmfully addictive. Rather than encouraging each other to take steps towards managing their emotions or solve their problems, they each stoke their fires, encouraging themselves that their righteous indignation is justified and that there is nothing wrong with it.

Yes, it feels good to let go of the negative emotions that you have been bottling up inside of you, but if that is all that you do you will find yourself back to overthinking and start bottling emotions up all over again; you still have no idea why you are in pain, and you have no idea about who is at fault.

Ignoring problems is bad, but also is taking self-awareness too far. People have become too introspective that even a twinge of sadness will trigger a rush of anxiety in them. Even minor mood swings are given great significance, and people feel the need to peer into them to discern their hidden meanings. Although some moods do hold messages, but most of the time their reasons are quite inconsequential, like the horrible traffic on the way to work, or because you did not get enough coffee. People have become so hypervigilant about their emotions, and that alone is enough to fuel endless nights of overthinking.

CHAPTER 2

CHALLENGING YOUR THOUGHTS

To stop overthinking, you need to first retrain your brain. Fortunately, there are many exercises and activities that you can use to reshape the way you think.

Now that you know a little about overthinking, and you also know when you are on the verge of dropping into that deep whirlpool of infinite negative emotions, you can start getting rid of it entirely, and you can start by challenging your thoughts before they run out of control.

Before You Begin

Here are some of the things that you need to know before you start challenging your negative thoughts so you will not get too surprised and overwhelmed with everything that is happening.

1. You need to know that challenging your thoughts might feel unnatural, sometimes even forced at first. But with a bit of practice, it will start to feel natural and believable.

2. To build up your confidence for thought challenging, you should practice them on thoughts that are not as upsetting and provides a bit more flexibility. It is also a good idea to practice this technique when you are still feeling a bit neutral and not too overwhelmed by your thoughts. Trying to practice thought challenging after a particularly rough and problematic day would be asking too much from yourself.

3. The first couple of times you try thought challenging it would be best if you jot down your responses. Often, when beginners try doing it in their heads, they end up with their thoughts going around in circles, which makes their thoughts all the more intense, and might cause them to spiral into overthinking.

4. Another benefit of taking down notes is that if a similar thought pops up in the future, you can refer to your notes and find out how you reacted to it.

5. You can practice with a family member or a friend whom you know will not judge you. Practicing with another person might help you by shedding light on the blind spots of your thinking, or they can offer you different viewpoints that you might find useful.

6. When you are first practicing thought challenging, you should focus on a single thought instead of a series of them this early in the game. For instance, instead of thinking "It's pretty obvious that my bosses thought I messed up the project" you should break down your thoughts into smaller, simpler sentences, and then challenge these thoughts one by one. You will only be confusing yourself if you start challenging a pile of thoughts at the same time.

7. Do something that will distract yourself once you finish working through a couple of thought challenging questions. This will give you some time for your mind to settle down.

Now that you know what you should expect, here are some of the most popular thought challenging exercise that you can try now.

Step Back and Assess the Situation

Here's a scenario that you might have experienced: you feel as if your boss is constantly and intentionally ignoring you. You think that the reason why your boss did not greet you this morning is because you somehow messed up something and that he is contemplating on firing you very soon. Usually, this kind of thoughts will cause your mind to overthink and cause you to lose sleep, thus causing you to not be as efficient at work, which therefore leads to you getting fired; in short, overthinking problems turns them into self-fulfilling prophecies.

On the other hand, if you just step back and analyze your thoughts before your overactive brain blows it way out of proportion, you can control it better. In the case mentioned above, remind yourself that your boss rarely greets anyone at all, and whatever screw up you might have made during the past couple of days is not grounds for your termination. Next, think about what you could do in order to not get fired, like increasing your productivity, or maybe learn a new skill that can help you do your job better.

In just a couple of minutes, you have derailed your train of negative thought before it even gets a chance to gain momentum.

Write Them All Down

Another way to challenge your negative thoughts before they trigger you to overthink is to write them all down on a piece of paper. When you write down the things that are bothering you, it gives them a somewhat tangible form, which actually helps you reanalyze them in a more rational manner. If you want to take this to the next level, you can start making a thought journal.

What is a thought journal/diary?

A thought diary is different from the traditional form of journaling, it has a structure that you have to follow to make analyzing your thoughts much easier. For instance, in a thought diary, you do not start an entry with a "Dear Diary" or any form of it, the entries look more like a ledger if anything.

You make a thought diary by making a couple of columns on the page and then you title them as follows:

Antecedent – These are the things that triggered you during the day.

Beliefs – These are your thoughts about the things that you listed in the first column.

Consequences – These are the things that happened because of your thoughts.

This is why a thought journal is called an ABC journal.

Here is an example on how you write an entry in your thought journal. You suddenly start worrying because you have an upcoming bill that you have to pay, this is your consequence. On the second column, you write that you were worried because you might not be able to make your due date. On the trigger section, you could write that you were watching the evening news when you suddenly remembered that you needed to pay.

After some time of writing in your thoughts journal, you might start noticing that the triggers are usually not related to the thoughts that made you worry. Thoughts just occur, and the triggers that caused them to surface might be related to them at all; thoughts are fickle in that way.

In the consequences column, you then might write down something like, "I took an aspirin to get rid of the headache that I felt was coming."

Every Sunday evening you could review your entries and then think of the things that you could have done better. For instance, for the entry above, instead of taking an aspirin, you could have just walked around the park to clear your mind, or at the very least you could have eaten an apple or something just so your headache will not get any worse. Or you could call your utility company and inform them that you might be a little late on the payment, but you will be paying, and ask if it is possible for them to waive the late fees. Your thought diary will help you make sense of your muddled thoughts by laying them out on paper for you to easily analyze. This tool can help you understand your less-than-ideal coping skills and why you end up making choices that lead to consequences that are not really best for you. With the help of a thought journal you can change your future consequences by restating and reanalyzing your past thoughts and making the necessary adjustments.

Benefits of a thought diary

Writing in a thought journal/diary helps you identify the things that trigger you into overthinking. When you write down your thoughts, you will easily see if they are actually legitimate concerns, or if they are just irrational. Thought journals help you recall how you behaved during the time you were triggered into overthinking, and in time you will start to notice the patterns in the way you think.

When you recognize your existing thought patterns, it will be possible for you to change not only your behavior, but also your thoughts. When you notice evil thoughts start to creep in, you can practice mindfulness (more on this later) and just observe and acknowledge them so they will go away. You actually do not need to behave according to your thoughts, you can actually ignore them and just continue living your own life. It is much better to write down "I ignored the thought of..." instead of "I went to the pub and drank a few pints to make myself forget", and if you notice that you are doing basically the same thing almost every day then your thought diary is actually working.

Make a habit of writing a thought journal

It is highly advisable that you make a habit out of writing down your thoughts using the format mentioned above. You can use a small notebook, a stack of papers, anything that you can write on and keep confidential. No one else aside from you and your therapist (if you are seeing one) must know about the existence of this journal; no one else should have access to your inner thoughts.

If you do not want to use the traditional method, you can also use your smartphone or laptop to create a secret document. Gradually over time, you will start noticing when you are starting to spiral into overthinking and then stop yourself from going any further.

Negative emotions, like those that shatter your confidence to pieces, can usually lead to clinical depression, makes you feel irrationally lonely, hopeless, and they will break you apart from the inside. Writing helps you get rid of your self-destructive thoughts. It is an art that can help you share your innermost feelings and your deepest thoughts.

Writing down your feelings onto paper is a way for you to freely express your views and opinions on the things that happened during the day, and what effect they had on your life. You are not just writing words on paper, you are effectively eliminating all these negative thoughts from your mind, and with them goes all that negativity that came with them.

Get a Hobby

Have you always wanted to learn to play the piano, the guitar, ukulele, or any other kind of musical instrument, why not try learning today? Do you want to get good at drawing, calligraphy, or painting? Attend classes or watch online video tutorials. You can also play your favorite video games for an hour or so. Having a hobby not only gives you a creative outlet, they also provide you with a way to create something with your hands, it also allows you to think individually, and most importantly, hobbies provide you with an escape from your negative thoughts.

Whenever you feel as if your thoughts are starting to overwhelming you, whip out your hobby kit, and immerse yourself in the activity. Lose yourself in the skills, coordination, concentration, and repetition that your hobby requires you to do. Focus your mind on the comfort or challenge brought about by your chosen hobby, and allow it to chase away all of the worries that used to trigger your overthinking.

Meditate Your Worries Away

Meditation can actually help you focus your mind away from the things that are troubling you. In fact, guided meditation can help you reset your mind, thus leaving you unburdened, and refreshed; ready for all the challenges that may come your way.

Meditation is different from mindfulness; the latter is a spur of the moment technique that you can use anywhere and anytime. Meditation, in the purest sense, should be practiced in a calm, silent, and relaxing environment as much as possible.

Here are a couple of meditation techniques. Give them all a try and choose the one that you vibe the most with.

1. *Focused breathing*

Breathing is one of the body's involuntary actions, meaning you do not really need to command your body to breath, it just happens. However, you can turn your breathing into a form of meditation just by taking notice of every breath that you take.

In focused breathing meditation, you take long, slow, deep breaths; breaths so deep that you fill your abdomen with air as well. To practice this form of meditation, you disengage your mind from all thoughts, and focus all your attention on your breathing. This is especially helpful for when you start noticing that your thoughts are starting to go out of your control.

However, this technique might not be appropriate for those who have respiratory ailments, like asthma and some heart ailments.

2. Body Scan

This technique is a combination of breath focus and muscle relaxation techniques. You first start by taking a couple of deep breaths, once you start feeling a bit relaxed focus your mind on one part of your body, or a group of muscles. For instance, focus on the fingers on your left foot, notice all of the sensations that each toe is feeling, and then mentally release any physical tension you have there. After which, focus on another set of muscles.

Doing a body scan not only makes you feel more relaxed, it also helps boost your awareness of your mind and body. However, if you recently got surgery that has a significant affect on your body image, or if you have body dysmorphic disorder, this technique might do more harm than good.

3. Guided Meditation

This technique requires you to come up with soothing scenery, places, or experiences that might help you relax better. If you have difficulty thinking up scenes for your guided meditation sessions, you can use any one of the many free apps available online.

Guided imagery is great because you just need to follow the instructions of the smooth voiced instructor and you will be alright. This technique is best for those who suffer from chronic intrusive thoughts.

4. Mindfulness Meditation

As mentioned earlier, this is different from actual meditation. This practice require only that you are sitting comfortably, and then focusing on the present without drifting towards your troubling thoughts of the past and the future. This form is presently enjoying quite a surge of popularity mainly because it can help people who are struggling with anxiety, chronic pain, and depression.

5. *Yoga, Tai Chi, or Qui Gong*

These three ancient arts might not seem similar, however, they all combine rhythmic breathing with different postures and body movements. The fact that you have to focus on your breathing while engaged in different poses make these activities effective at distracting your mind away from your negative thoughts. In addition, these exercises can also help you gain more flexibility, balance, and core strength. However, if you have a debilitating or painful condition that prevents you from doing anything remotely physical, then these activities might not be right for you. However, you can still ask your physician if you can practice these exercises, he might recommend a good physical therapist or gym that can actually help you. Now, if your doctor believes that it is a bad idea for you to do these exercises, heed his words and look elsewhere for a solution.

6. *Repetitive Prayers/Chants*

This technique is best for those who have relatively short attention spans, so much so that they have trouble focusing on their breath. For this technique, you recite a short prayer, or even a phrase or two from a prayer while focusing on your breath. This method might be more appealing to you if you are religious or if you are a particularly spiritual person.

If you are not religious, or you do not subscribe to any religion, you can do this by replacing the prayers/chants with positive affirmations or lines from your favorite poem.

Psychological experts advise not just choosing one technique out of the list mentioned above. It is much better to try as many of them as you can and then stick to the one/s that you find effective. It is also recommended that you practice these techniques for at least 20 minutes a day for best results, although even just a couple of minutes of practice can help. However, the longer and more often you practice these techniques, the greater the benefits and stress reduction.

CHAPTER 3

---- ≋ ----

FOCUSING ON ACTIVE PROBLEM SOLVING

One of the absolute best ways to deal with your overthinking disorder is to focus more on active problem solving rather than dwelling on the things that make you worry. When you focus on solving the problems at hand, you will not only distract yourself from the negative thoughts that came with your problems, you also prevent them from coming back to trouble you again.

Active Problem Solving Defined

As mentioned earlier, it is a better use of your energy and time to just focus on solving the problem at hand rather than reining in the emotions that they stirred up from inside of you. Ruminating on your problems does nothing to solve them, what they do is make you feel even worse and sorry for yourself; nothing gets accomplished and the problem still remains.

On the other hand, when you take on the problem head-on, you feel empowered; you no longer feel that your life is in shambles. You start to believe that your life is manageable and not as stress-filled as you first thought it was.

Active problem solving is immediately taking on the things that worry you and then taking care of the root problem, instead of letting the ghost go and leave everything unresolved. However, active problem solving is easier said than done.

Sometimes, facing problems directly is almost impossible because doing so means you will be on a head-on collision with your fears, possible conflicts, and your feelings of awkwardness. Fortunately, it does get easy over time. The amount of discomfort you will feel will gradually reduce because you know that you will no longer have a problem looming over your head once you are done solving it.

When is It Best to Use Active Problem Solving?

It is best that you learn this early on: active problem solving is not appropriate for all situations. Some situations are deemed unsolvable; there are some circumstances that are simply beyond your control, like the weather, how other people would react, and many others.

Take this scenario for instance: your sister is dating someone whom you do not particularly like, and you heard that the two of them are already engaged and plans on getting married soon. This decision of your sister caused you to feel anger and sadness. In this situation, you cannot apply active problem solving because you have no say on who your sister wants to marry, and the only thing that you can do now is to learn to cope using your emotion-centric skills.

Here is another scenario: you are arguing with your landlord because the heat in your apartment somehow got cut off, and you have been wearing a thick jacket indoors for three days now. In this case, though you still need to use emotion-focused coping skills in order to get your anger back in check, but you will mostly be using active problem solving to resolve your issue with your landlord. You need to resolve this problem, or else you will be overthinking all throughout the night in a very cold apartment.

How to Implement Active Problem Solving

There are 5 steps in the Active Problem Solving process:

Step 1 – Identify the problem

This is where you analyze your situation and then you figure out what is the root cause of all your troubles.

In the example above, your main problem is that the heat in your apartment is on the fritz, and your landlord is not doing anything to fix it. The problem is not that your air conditioning is on the fritz, the real problem is the inaction of your landlord to solve your problem.

Step 2 – List all possible solutions

Sit down and come up with a list of all the possible solutions that you can use to solve your problem. Write down everything that you can come up with, it does not matter if it seems far fetched right now, every idea has the potential to help.

Now that you have the actual problem on hand, and you also have a list of potential answers. In the example above, some of the possible answers could be to storm the apartment of your landlord, knock down his door and demand that he fix the heat in your apartment. On the other hand, you can do some research on tenant's rights in your area, and then write your landlord a gracious letter requesting that he fix the HVAC in your apartment (you do not have to resort to threats just yet). Or, you could write a letter that actually DEMANDS that your landlord fix the heating or you will sue him for your inconvenience.

Step 3 – Evaluate each option and select the best choice

Now that you have a list of the possible things that you can do, evaluate each one of them, and find out which one is the most viable course of action. Imagine what would happen if you went with a particular course of action. Will there be negative repercussions if you chose this particular plan? Worst-case scenario: if every one of your plans seem unlikely to succeed, which one would hurt you the least?

In the hypothetical case between you and your landlord over the broken heating, all three of the possible solutions are viable, but only one of them could result in minimal repercussions. The second option, the one where you write a courteous letter of intent to your landlord, would be the best course of action because you do not risk having your landlord hate you, which will come in handy when you negotiate your lease for the following year. However, you still need to watch your back and have a received copy of the letter just in case the whole thing goes south.

Finding out which one is the most viable course of action can be quite tricky, especially since you might feel biased towards the choices that are not as difficult to do. In this case, it is best to run your choices to other people, like your friends, or better yet, with a lawyer so that you will know if you yourself are breaking any rules.

Step 4 – Take action

Once you have decided on a plan, immediately put it into action. This is not the time to second guess yourself (in fact, do not second guess yourself as it will trigger your overthinking disorder), jump right into the thick of it and implement your plan. It might seem difficult, but think of it as if it was a Band-aid; it would be better for you to just rip it off in one fell swoop rather than taking it slow and prolonging your agony.

During this step, ask yourself the following questions: when will you implement your plan (writing down the exact date is the best), and who will you talk to regarding this problem.

Back to the previous problem. When will you send your landlord the letter of intent? If possible, you should send it as soon as you can, or else risk days of freezing nights. As to who you need to talk to, that would be your landlord, and if possible, you should also consult with a legal expert so that you will know what to do in case your landlord remains stoic about not fixing your apartment. If all goes well, your heat will be back on in no time.

Step 5 – Does this solve your problem?

After all has been said and done, did the process solve your problem? Did you only get a partial solution, and the bulk of the problem is still there? Did things get even more complicated now? If you did not get the ideal outcome, or the result was not even worth considering as a success, go back to the third step and try again.

Let us take into consideration that your landlord still refused to fix the problem with your heating; this means you have to go back to step 3, which is evaluating the possible courses of action and choosing which one to go with. In this case, since option 2 failed, the next most viable solution is option 3, which is to write a letter informing your landlord that you will be suing him for violating your right as a tenant, citing which specific laws he broke, and that you have hired the services of a competent lawyer.

This time, what outcome did you get? If you did your research well, and you documented every piece of paper that were sent back and forth between the two parties, then you will have an ironclad case on your hands. Your landlord will have no other choice but to fix your heating, and since he already know that you are aware of your tenant's rights, he will make sure that no further violations will be happening in the future.

If you are persistent, you will most likely solve your problem, and in the event that you do, you'll have:

a) Gotten rid of the problem and the emotions associated to it

b) Became more self-confident because you can tackle difficult issues like this

So, regardless if you had a lot of trouble solving the problem and it took you awhile, or if your plan went without nary a hitch and you solved the problem on your first try, you will still get a couple of bonuses once you cross the finish line.

CHAPTER 4

PRACTICING MINDFULNESS

When you overthink, you detach yourself from the present moment. You become blissfully unaware of where you are, and what you are doing, it's as if you are on auto-pilot, but the thing is that you are only going around in circles. If you are a chronic overthinker, you need to find a way to snap yourself out of this vicious thought cycle before it sucks you in deeper, and this is where mindfulness can help.

Actually, mindfulness practice is not just for snapping you out of your overthinking habit, it can actually minimize the times you overthink, and maybe even eliminate this bad habit entirely.

What is Mindfulness?

If this is the first time you encountered the term "mindfulness", it is similar to meditation, but at the same time it is different as well. There are some concepts that are shared between the two practices, but they are not that many. Being mindful is being aware, but not judgmental, of what you are currently experiencing (including your thoughts and emotions) in the present moment. It being aware of yourself and your present moment. You might think that you are already naturally aware of yourself, but you will learn that it is actually a skill that you are still yet to develop.

Most people live their lives the way their thinking minds and egos dictate them. Some researchers call this unconscious perspective as the person's Default Mode Network, or DMN for short. Your DMN filters your present perceptions based on your past experiences, recurring habits, and any and all beliefs and/or opinions that you have developed in your life; the problem here is that it does not discern if the information it got is true or not. In order to be aware about the truth of the thoughts in your mind, you need to practice mindfulness.

People spend a majority of their time living as the voice that is inside their heads, and that voice is constantly analyzing and judging everything, and is always blabbbering about useless stuff, and they often come with distracting mental images so they can hold onto their attention rather than let them take notice of what is really happening around them.

The truth is that everyone is conditioned to always be detachcd from the present. Do you think that you are better than most people? If you think so then you are most likely not. People who believe that they are not conditioned to act, think, and decide according to their habits and past experiences are the one who are more prone to overthinking and detaching from the present. These people are blissfully unaware of their conditioning, which leads to them living an "unconscious" life.

What is mindfulness?

Mindfulness is a person's ability to be fully present in the moment; it is being aware of where you are and what you are currently doing, but also not being overly reactive or easily overwhelmed by the things that are going on around you. And although mindfulness is something that is naturally within every person, it becomes more effective when it is practiced every day.

When you make yourself aware to what you are experiencing by using your senses, or to your state of mind by analyzing your thoughts and feelings, you are being mindful. There are actually quite a number of medical research that shows that with consistent mindfulness training, you are actually remolding the physical structure of your brain.

With this in mind (pardon the pun), the goal of mindfulness is to make yourself aware of the intricacies of your mental, emotional, and physical processes. It is basically you learning more about yourself.

What is Meditation?

When you meditate, you let your mind wander; there is no fixed destination, there are no finish lines to tell you when to stop, you just go where you want to go. Unbeknownst to many, meditating does not mean that your brain will be devoid of any and all thoughts, it does not completely eliminate distractions, it does not turn you into an empty vessel. Meditating is like you going to your special place where every second of every moment receives special treatment. When you are meditating, you venture into the innermost workings of your mind, you are more in touch with your senses (you notice the air blowing on your skin, you get a waft of the flowers on the mantle, etc.), your emotions (you love feeling this way, or you hate it, you crave for something, etc.), and with your thoughts (this is where you notice your irrational thoughts that trigger overthinking).

Mindfulness only asks that you suspend judgment and for once become curious about how your mind works; and you do so with kindness, both to yourself and to others.

What Mindfulness Is NOT

Before you start learning more about mindfulness practice, you need to get the records straight about it. Here are five things that people usually get wrong about mindfulness:

1. Mindfulness will not "fix" you

If you are suffering from any form of mental illness, be warned that mindfulness cannot cure you, nor does it claim to. Mindfulness can only help you deal with the symptoms, but it cannot fix the underlying ailment.

2. Mindfulness is not about stopping your thoughts or clearing your mind

When you practice mindfulness, you are not shutting down your brain. You are not emptying your mind of all thought. In fact, you are only actually acknowledging all of the unwanted thoughts in your mind so they can leave on their own. When you finish meditating, your thoughts are still in your head, but they will not be bothering you as much, and most of them are on their way out.

3. Mindfulness does not belong to any religion or sect

Anyone can practice mindfulness. Christians, Muslims, even atheists can all practice mindfulness. No one religion claims to have exclusive rights to meditating, you can practice meditation regardless if you are religious or not. You can also include some aspects of your belief into your meditation; for instance, if you are a devout Catholic, you can use prayers to meditate, or if you are a Buddhist, you can use mantras to get into the right headspace.

4. Mindfulness does not help you escape from reality

Just like how it does not help empty your mind, mindfulness also does not let you escape from reality. What many people thought about meditation is actually false. For instance, you cannot escape the real world and escape to a "happy place" in your mind. The truth is that mindfulness actually makes you more aware of the things that are happening around you, which is the polar opposite. Escaping to a "happy place" is only a stop-gap solution, when you get out of your happy place your problems are still in the real world.

5. Mindfulness is not a panacea

Mindfulness is not, nor has it ever claimed to be a cure-all for anything that ails you. If you are suffering from any sort of medical condition, you should seek treatment from a medical doctor, do not rely on mindfulness to let you "think" your sickness away. Many have tried to "fix" themselves this way, and most, if not all, of them have failed miserably. Meditation is just like a maintenance medication of sorts, it aids in proper treatment, but it is not the main treatment.

Why You Need to Practice Mindfulness

You can practice mindfulness in every moment. You can either choose to meditate and perform body scans in a quiet room, or for instance, when your phone rings, you can pause and take a deep breath before answering it. To make you even more motivated to practice mindfulness, here are some of its benefits:

It Turns You Into A Better Decision-maker

One of the main problems of making a habit out of DMN is that you think that you only have limited choices to make decisions. Rather than considering if something can be good (or bad), you just act on whatever things might come by default. The more you subject yourself to this habit of yours, the more ingrained in your mind it becomes, until such time comes when you do it without even thinking about your best interests. Even just two weeks of mindfulness practice can greatly reduce instances of wandering minds and it also helped people improve their focus. In addition, mindfulness empowers people to be more creative and clear when making decisions, especially those concerning their finances.

Mindfulness also trains your mind to work more efficiently. Researchers compared the brains scans of mindfulness practitioners to a control group. The results showed that the mindfulness group had more executive control, in other words, they are better decision-makers. The practitioners also had better mental acuity according to tests done after they practice mindfulness.

It Provides You With A Place Where You Can Be Free From Conditioning

How many times have you watched the evening news and there always seem to be at least one news item that grinds your gears. It is quite unfortunate that most people go through life reactively. Mindfulness provides you with awareness and a space in your head that allows you to choose how to respond, rather than having a knee-jerk reaction to things. You get a chance to choose your reaction rather than letting your mind default to the kinds of reactions that society has ingrained into you.

It Allows You To Increase Your Emotional Intelligence

Have you ever been angry at someone and then later regretted lashing out on that person? How many times have you started crying and then immediately regretted it because you could not stop? Are you easily startled by even the smallest thing? Do you have a nasty habit of losing your temper? If you think that your emotions are starting to take over your life, you need to practice mindfulness.

Medical studies have shown that people who practice mindfulness have better control over their emotions compared to other people. In fact, the US Military conducted their own research on mindfulness and how it could help sufferers of PTSD. Their research yielded that mindfulness can actually help minimize stress, and even ease the effects of chronic stress.

Mindfulness practice also helps people deal with change much better, become less dependent on the opinions of others, and also become more resilient when it comes to facing unpleasant emotions. Practicing mindfulness creates a bit of space between you and your emotions so you will have more time to process them and react to them accordingly.

Mindfulness training not only makes you more mature emotionally, you also gain more empathy, compassion, and you also become more altruistic. After even just eight weeks, you will feel more empathy with others, and you are also more able to take compassionate action.

It Helps Your Body Thrive

Lots of athletes from all over the world use mindfulness to improve their performance. University basketball players practice mindfulness to help them accept their negative thoughts so they will not get nervous during the game, surfers practice mindfulness so they can get a hold of their fears and ride those humongous waves.

Mindfulness can also increase the amount of physical activity that your body can endure. Most people distract themselves from their workouts, but it is actually better when you practice mindfulness while you are working out. For instance, if you are in a hurry to finish your weight training workout, you will only focus on doing the requisite number of repetitions, and not pay attention to your form. And when you are not careful about your lifting form, you are more prone to getting seriously injured. With mindfulness, not only are you careful about your weightlifting form, you will also feel more accomplished with every set that you complete.

It Helps You Become More Creative

Regardless if it is with writing, drawing, sculpting, and other arts, you can use mindfulness to increase your creativity.

Creativity arises from the DMN. In these periods of unfocused rest you have the chance to have a different perspective, you can make new associations between ideas and strike upon them. For instance, if you are a sculptor, you do not immediately know what to carve out of a huge chunk of stone. You need to sit in front of that huge slab of stone, and visualize what you can make out of it. The only way to see the final sculpture clearly is to eliminate all distractions around you.

The greatest obstacle to your creativity are the distractions that are around you. When your mind is distracted, it cannot switch from the its task-positive mode back to the DMN, which leads you to getting stuck in a rut. To make things worse, these distractions come in many different forms, from your regular daily tasks, to the different ongoing stressors that you have to deal with (like relationship and money problems).

With mindfulness, you can say goodbye to all of your distractions, and say hello to an almost infinite source of inspiration.

It Helps Strengthen Existing Neural Connections and Build New Ones

Remember earlier when it was mentioned that mindfulness can actually reshape the human brain, it meant in terms of creating new neural connections. Practicing mindfulness as often as you can will cause your brain to build new neural pathways, and ultimately new neural networks, thus making it function more efficiently. This helps your brain by improving concentration and awareness.

What Do You Need to Do to be More Mindful?

Practice mindfulness ad nauseam. There is no shortcut or magic pill that will help you become instantly more mindful. This book does not promise instant results, although you will receive tips that will make the process much easier, but it will still take you some time before you can become fully mindful. Being mindful means that you are training your mind to be aware of what it is thinking, rather than becoming what it is actually thinking.

This is where meditation can help you. There are many ways to meditate, the traditional method of sitting in a quiet place and observing your thoughts without being judgmental is the easiest way, and is also the best place to start for beginners. It might sound simple, but the problem is that most people are not living in the present, they are constantly worrying about things that are yet to happen, or happened already. Your thoughts are constantly running around uncontrolled in your brain. With mindfulness, you can put a bit of space around your thoughts so you can easily let go of comparisons, judgments, and control of them.

The Basics of Mindfulness-Based

Now, you will be learning how you can actually practice mindfulness. Here are some ways that you can help tune your mind into becoming more mindful every day:

Set aside time for practice. The great thing about mindfulness practice is that you do not need a fancy meditation cushion, or any other special equipment. However, you do need to set aside some time in your day for practicing mindfulness.

Observe the now. As mentioned earlier, mindfulness is not about silencing your thoughts, nor is it about attaining absolute inner peace. The ultimate goal of mindfulness is to train your mind to pay attention to the present moment, all without being judgmental of it; and this is easier said than done.

Let your judgments pass you by. Speaking of being judgmental, whenever you do notice that you are beginning to judge your views of the now, just take a mental note of your judgmental thoughts, and then let them drift past you.

Go back to observing the now. One cannot be mindful all the time, but one can return back to being mindful anytime. You cannot help it if your mind gets carried away sometime, especially when you are lost deep in your thoughts, but with mindfulness, you can drag yourself back into observing the now.

Be kind to your mind. Removing judgment is not just for your thoughts, you should also extend the same courtesy to your mind as well. Do not judge yourself if ever some irrational thoughts pop into your head, things like this happen all the time. The important thing is that you recognize when these things happen, and gently bring your mind back to the present.

Get a change of scenery. When you start to feel worried, get up and move to a new location. Not that many people are aware that their environment can also affect their moods. If you start feeling anxious while you are in a quiet room, go to where there is a bit more life. If you are getting overwhelmed by noise and too much energy, go somewhere quiet. The idea here is to disrupt your thoughts by giving it new sensations to process.

Do something to get your creative juices flowing. Creativity has a different way of using your brain compared to how it is used by doing mundane tasks. Do not think that you are not creative, or that you do not have the talent for anything; everyone is creative, and that includes you of course. The problem is that you shut out your creative side because you feel that you are not good enough, or that it is just a waste of your time. Creativity is more than just the end-product, it is the entire process. Do not worry if you do not produce something that is beautiful in the broad sense, just create things that you can be proud of.

Get moving. One of the best things that you can do to fix your worried mind is to get a bit more physical. When you exercise your brain releases endorphins, these are brain chemicals that will make you feel happier, more relaxed, and less stressed.

Use your strengths. When you do something that you know you are good at, it is almost impossible not to feel good. It is never a bad thing to try something new, but if you feel as if you are starting to struggle and you are beginning to feel a bit overwhelmed, do something that you know you excel at. For instance, if you are a good baker, whip up a batch of your favorite muffins or cookies. Are you great at gardening? Putter around in your garden for a bit, maybe even pick a couple of flowers so you have something refreshing on your work desk. These activities will help you snap out of your funk and get back to living in the now.

Distract yourself by doing something that uses brainpower. Distraction is one way to easily rid yourself of anxiety and worry. However, some types of distractions are better than others. For instance, for some people, binge-watching their favorite series on Netflix is a great way to deal with their anxious minds, but there are also some people who cannot shut their brain even if they are watching TV. If you are one of them, you can try other activities that require a bit more thinking and reasoning, like a Sudoku puzzle, a crossword puzzle, or trying your hand at a rather complicated craft that you saw online.

Make use of all your senses. An effective way to ground yourself back into the present is by using all of your senses to notice what is in front of you. Notice how many windows there are inside the room? Can you smell something cooking in the kitchen? How does the cushion on your chair feel? Can you hear that slight humming sound coming from the AC? Doing this engages your brain and distracts it from your worries, which then immediately grounds you back into the present.

Breathe deeply. The great thing about breathing exercises to deal with anxiety and worry is that you can do it anywhere you like. There are many breathing exercises that you can try, and all of them are readily available online. However, all that you need to do is to slow down your breathing and focus on inhaling and exhaling. Count to five when you inhale and notice your chest rise, and then count to five as you exhale and notice your chest drop. Not only does focusing on your breath bring you back to the present, the increased amount of oxygen in your system also helps calm you down.

A Simple Mindfulness Meditation Practice for Beginners

If this is your first time to try meditation then you might feel a bit anxious and nervous that you might do it wrong and thus negate its effects; don't. There is absolutely no way that you can mess up with mindfulness meditation, you do not even need to follow the proceeding instructions to the letter, do with it as you want, the effects will still be relatively the same.

1. *Sit in a comfortable position.* It does not matter where you sit (on the floor, on a chair, on your couch, and others) as long as you are comfortable then that is fine. Just make sure that you are sitting on something that is stable and comfy.

2. *Take notice of what your legs are doing.* If you are sitting cross-legged on a cushion, notice how your legs intertwine and which parts are experiencing more pressure than others. If you are on a chair, notice how the bottoms of your feet lie flat on the floor.

3. *Keep your back straight.* You should keep your back as straight as you can, however, do not stiffen up. Your

backbone has a natural curvature, so let it rest in that position.

4. *Take note of what your arms are doing.* Position your arms in such a way that your upper arms are more or less parallel to your upper body, and place your palms on your legs anywhere you feel most comfortable.

5. *Soften your gaze.* Tilt your head a bit downward and let your gaze follow. You do not have to close your eyes. You can just let your eyes fall where they want. If there are objects in front of your eyes, just let them be there, do not focus on them.

6. *Feel your breath.* Point your thoughts toward your breath. Take notice of the air moving into your nose and going out of your mouth, and the rising of your chest with every breath.

7. *Keep an eye out for the times when your attention sways away from your breath.* There will always be times when your mind will wander away from your breath, do not worry when this happens. You do not have to block or avoid your thoughts, just gently coax your mind back to focusing on your breath.

8. *Take it easy on your mind.* You might find your mind constantly wander while you are meditating, do not be too hard on yourself, this kind of thing happens all the time. Instead of fighting your thoughts, you should practice just observing them, do not judge them and do not react to them, and just sit there and pay attention to your breath.

9. *When you are ready, lift your gaze.* When you are ready (do not worry because you will know when you are ready), take a moment to notice any sounds around you. Notice all of the sensations that your body is feeling, and then take notice of your thoughts and your emotions.

You just finished your first mindfulness meditation, that was not so bad now wasn't it? Again, you do not have to follow the instructions to the last detail, just as long as you feel the way you should then you did just fine.

CHAPTER 5

DEALING WITH PROCRASTINATION

Is there really a connection between overthinking and procrastination? Why yes, there is, and it is actually more harmful than your garden-variety procrastination. Procrastination as a result of overthinking is called "analysis paralysis", this means you have so many thoughts running through your mind at once that you cannot pick just one. You have to pick apart every option that you have until you are satisfied, which rarely is the case (overthinkers usually never come to a conclusive choice).

This is one of the ugliest facets of overthinking that does not really get too much attention, mainly because people do not equate procrastination with overthinking and anxiety; they believe that procrastination is just a byproduct of laziness, and that is sadly not the case.

What is Analysis Paralysis?

Before going deeper into this harmful habit, consider the ancient fable about the Fox and the Cat. The Fox and the Cat were talking in the forest, the Fox said "I can never be caught by the hunters because I have hundreds of ideas on how I can easily escape them!" The cat, who is a bit jealous, said "You are so lucky, I only know one way to escape capture." Upon hearing this, the fox just gloated and chided the cat for not being as smart as he is.

Suddenly, in the distance, the pair heard the bawling of a group of hunting hounds. The cat quickly clambered up the tallest tree he could find so he can escape. The fox, on the other hand, just stood there contemplating which of his hundred or so escape ideas he should use today; he got so engrossed in his thoughts that the hunters' hounds caught up to him and captured the bewildered Fox. Originally, the lesson of the story is to not let your hubris cloud your judgment, but it can also be used as a classic example of the dangers of Analysis Paralysis.

Analysis paralysis, as the name suggests, is the state of over-analyzing (or overthinking) situations so much that a clear decision or action is not taken, which leads to the paralysis of the outcome.

When a person is experiencing analysis paralysis, he gets so engrossed into the analyzing and evaluating of data need to make a correct decision, just like the fox in the fable, you will never reach the right choice, you will just be stuck there with your mouth agape and unable to take any form of action.

Analysis paralysis happens when one's fear of what could potentially go wrong is stronger than the actual realistic potential for success. This imbalance results in the suppression of a person's decision-making in an effort to preserve and try out other existing options. This surplus of available options can make the situation more overwhelming than it actually is and thus causing a sort of mental paralysis, which renders the person unable to make up his mind.

Analysis paralysis becomes an even bigger problem when a decision is direly needed in critical situations, but the person in charge cannot decide fast enough, thus resulting in an even bigger problem than before if only a fast decision was made.

Casual Analysis Paralysis

There are different forms of analysis paralysis, but there are two main distinctions: personal and conversational analysis paralysis.

Personal Analysis

Casual analysis paralysis can happen when you are trying to make a personal decision, but you cannot because you are overanalyzing the situation that you are currently facing. This happens when the sheer volume of information that you have to process starts to become too overbearing. You get so burdened by the amount of things in your head that you cannot, for the life of you, make a rational decision.

There are some cases wherein the decision-maker could successfully analyze every possible outcome, and even write them all down, but then inexplicably trash all of them because he did not like how he analyzed them. Not only is this a waste of mental and physical energy, it is also a waste of your time, which is not a good look when this often happens to you while you are at work.

Conversational Analysis

Analysis paralysis can happen at any time during any typical conversation, however, conversational analysis paralysis usually happens when discussing intellectual and heavy topics. During the course of an intellectual discussion, a person might over-analyze a specific issue, up to the point that the original subject of the conversation is lost. This usually happens because complex intellectual subjects are interconnected with other intellectual issues, and the pursuit of these other branches of discussion somehow makes logical sense to the participants. However, this actually does not make much sense because it muddles the conversation, and the topic of discussion strays so far from the original.

How Overthinking is Holding You Back

Delaying action while over-analyzing available information does not help with productivity. A 2010 survey done by LexisNexis (a legal research company) showed that employees spend more than half of their workday just receiving and analyzing information rather than doing their jobs. However, that is just what people see on the surface. Studies in the field of psychology and neuroscience showed that analysis paralysis takes a bigger toll on you than just wasting your time.

Here are some of the ways that analysis paralysis is holding you back:

1. Analysis paralysis negatively affects your performance on mentally-demanding tasks

Your working memory allows you to focus only on the information that you need to finish your tasks. Unfortunately, you only have a limited supply of working memory per day. Once you have used up all of your available working memory you cannot fit any more information in your brain.

Research showed that high-stress situations can lead to decreased performance when doing mentally-demanding tasks, these are the tasks that where you rely heavily on your working memory to finish. In addition, if there are more participants who want to perform well on a task, the more their performance suffers. Researchers believe that anxiety and stress produces distracting thoughts that take up a lot of your working memory that you could have used to work on your tasks.

2. Analysis paralysis eats at your willpower

A study published by the National Academy of Science looked at the decisions made by parole board judges within a 10-month period. The study found the judges were more likely to grant prisoners parole early in the morning and immediately after eating lunch. They were also more likely to deny parole when the cases are placed on their desk after the end of a particularly long work session. This phenomenon held true over the course of the study, a span that encompassed more than 1,100 cases, regardless of the severity of the crime, which makes it more than just a simple coincidence.

What could have explained these rather surprising, and disturbing discoveries? The judges suffered from what psychology professionals call "decision fatigue". Every decision that people make during the course of the day, like whether to hit the snooze button or not, having fish or chicken for lunch, and other times when you have to choose between several options, they all draw from a limited reserve of willpower. Imagine your willpower as if it was a muscle; the more you use it, the faster you wear it out, which then leaves you mentally exhausted and feeling overwhelmed. This is why dieters have no problem keeping up with their program when it is still early in the day and they are still relatively full after eating a healthy breakfast and lunch, but they are more likely to succumb to the temptation of eating junk food during their afternoon coffee break. During the course of the day the amount of willpower you will have left will dwindle, but it will replenish itself in the morning, only for you to repeat the cycle all over again.

The things that you do without thinking, like brushing your teeth, or putting on your clothes, take little to no willpower at all, so you can still somehow get through the day. However, when you take too long at making a decision, you are quickly depleting what little amount of willpower you have left in your mind.

When you are running low on willpower, your capability to make wise decisions are affected. This means you are more likely to choose to eat unhealthy food, skip exercising, and procrastinate working on your side projects. In short, when you over-analyze your decisions, making more difficult choices even harder in the long run.

3. When you overthink you become less happy

Back in 1956, Herman Simon, an economist, first coined the term "satisficer", which is basically a decision-making style that gives more weight to solutions that are just adequate rather than those that are optimal. Satisficers are people who will only decide once most, if not all of their criteria are met. For instance, they will only stay in a hotel if the in-house restaurant serves the kind of pasta that he wants.

In comparison, "maximizers" want to make the best possible decision. Even when they see something that meets their criteria, they will not make a decision until they have compared it with other possible options. They will waste a lot of their time and energy to find options, regardless if they have little or no significance to the actual task.

Regardless if you are a satisficer or a maximizer, research suggests that your behavior has a huge negative impact on your well-being. These studies found that:

Maximizers are significantly less satisfied, happy, optimistic, has less self-esteem, and has significantly more regrets compared to satisficers.

Maximizers are more prone to suffering from buyer's regret. They cannot help but compare themselves to others and engaging in counterfactual thinking. For instance, they immediately feel sad when they buy an item, they almost immediately think what would have happened if they chose the other item instead. Instead of happiness when they made a purchase, they just feel regret.

Maximizers are more likely to fall into a negative mood once they notice that they did not perform as well as their peers. It's like professional jealousy, but it also spills over to the person's personal life. They constantly compare themselves to people they know, and if they do not perceive themselves to be better than their peers, it will be reason enough to worry oneself into analysis paralysis.

Although analyzing every option available does lead to the absolute best outcome, maximizing will only lead to more stress, anxiety, regret, and you will still not be entirely happy when you do make a decision.

Okay, so now you know how overthinking any decision can and will only make you anxious, kills your productivity, and overall lowers your self-esteem, but what can you do to stop it?

Here are some simple ways that can help you stop over-analyzing your options, avoid getting trapped by analysis paralysis, and just start doing all the things that you are supposed to do:

1. Structure your day according to the decisions that are most important to you

Not all decisions are equal. For instance, deciding on a brand of toothpaste to buy later is less worthy of your limited supply of willpower compared to, say deciding on whether to agree to the terms of your suppliers or not.

Your ability to make quality decisions wane deteriorate with every choice you make throughout the day, regardless if said decisions are inconsequential or not. This is why you need to schedule your day so that you can minimize the number of decisions that you need to make every day. For instance, divide your workload so that you tackle your most important tasks first thing in the morning, while you still have a lot of willpower to spare. In addition, automate your small, insignificant decisions so that you do not have to waste energy on them. Take Mark Zuckerberg for instance, as head of the biggest social media network in the world, he cannot be bothered to waste energy deciding what clothes he needs to wear, so he wears the same grey t-shirt and jeans combo every day of the week, unless the occasion needs him to change.

Do not even try to tackle big decisions late in the afternoon, you will only drain whatever amount of willpower you have left in your body, and it will only make you feel overwhelmed, cranky, and regretful. If you find yourself getting caught in a downward spiral of overthinking and analysis paralysis, wrestle yourself out of it by doing something that is completely unrelated to your previous task; or better yet, call it a day. Just come back to the task the next morning when your willpower reserves are refilled.

2. Limit the amount of information you consume

There is a virtually limitless amount of information that you can consult for any sort of problem that you face. For instance, when you are writing a book report, you have an endless number of websites that you can go to for all the important information that you need to know. This is why you need to approach your research with solid intention.

Sherlock Holmes, the greatest literary detective to ever grace the pages of a book, is infamous for only consuming information that he could use in his profession. For instance, Holmes has little to no knowledge about Literature, Philosophy, and Politics, which are subjects that he deems unimportant to his profession. However, his skills in Botany, Human Anatomy, and Geology are variable, he only took various tidbits from the subjects to help him in his cases; for instance, regarding botany, Holmes has an extensive library of knowledge about poisonous plants, especially the ones from the belladonna family.

Holmes knows that the capacity of his brain is very limited so he only stores the information that he needs. Be like Sherlock Holmes, for your workday, only consume information that you will need to finish your tasks; turn off your smartphone, do not open your social media accounts, and do not open your personal email, do those things at the end of the day.

3. Set a deadline for yourself to make yourself accountable

According to Parkinson's Law, your work will expand to fill the space of time that you set aside for it. For instance, give yourself an hour to finish a task, and you will see that it will take exactly an hour. Give yourself 15 minutes to finish the same task and you could finish it within fifteen minutes. The same holds for decision-making; if you set a deadline for a decision, it will force you to make an efficient decision within that set amount of time.

However, tricking yourself to commit to a self-imposed deadline can be quite hard, but you should find a way that you can hold yourself accountable. One way to do this is to make your deadline as public as possible. Tell a co-worker that you gave yourself a deadline to finish your tasks, or better yet, announce in your social media accounts that you are giving yourself a deadline. The more people who know about your deadline, the better.

4. Stick to your main objective

Identifying your main objective and then sticking to it can help you overcome your tendency to fall into analysis paralysis.

All of your decisions should center around your main objective. If a decision does not affect your main objective in any way, set it aside for later. Only think about the things that you need to do to get closer to your main objective. Because you know your main objective, it helps you make quick and decisive choices because you can immediately assess the options available to you.

4. Talk with someone else so you can escape your own mind

People are naturally predisposed to overestimate just how unhappy they will be when something bad happens to them, and also overestimate just how happy they will be when things go their way. Studies have shown that complete strangers are actually better at predicting your own satisfaction or dissatisfaction from a decision that you yourself made.

Whenever you are bogged down by a decision that you have to make, just asking another person for his or her opinions about the subject will help you make a decision that you are actually okay with, as compared to making the decision yourself without other people's input.

The next time you find yourself overthinking over a singular important issue, ask a co-worker if you could bother him or her for a minute or so, or you can consult with your supervisor, or if you have one, your mentor. When you present your deliberations to other people, you are actually forcing yourself to synthesize the information in a more clear and concise manner (compared to how muddled and messy the information was when it was still in your mind).

In addition, having someone else validate your ideas, especially if that someone is a person whom you respect, might just be the thing that you need to get over your self-doubt and gain enough confidence to take further action.

5. Approach problems with an iterative mindset.

Of course, it is more difficult to make a sound decision when your uncertainty is at its peak. Usually, people base their choices on personal assumptions that may, or may not be all that accurate. To compensate, people would do a lot of unnecessary research to convince themselves that their choice is right. However, the only true way to find out is to actually take action.

Fortunately, there is an easier way that you can test your assumptions without completely committing yourself to a specific path of action; this is called the iterative approach. This is a concept that has its roots in software development, but you can also use in your day-to-day decision making.

The basic idea of the iterative approach is to not waste a lot of time coming up with a perfect product, instead focus on producing the most "minimum viable product" and release it to a limited group of testers. This will help you gain much needed feedback that you can use to tweak your "product" quickly and efficiently. You are basically getting other people to help you figure out the problems in your choices before you can actually commit to a final decision. You can do this as many times as needed, with every iteration of your "product" getting better than the one before it, until you can come up with the final release version.

Using the iterative method also has the added benefit of helping you break out of analysis paralysis. Viewing your decision as final will only bring a lot of unneeded pressure and stress, thus causing you to overthink and overanalyze every available option that you can choose. With the iterative approach, you view your decisions as experiments that you can draw conclusions from and therefore make the next iteration better. There is no stress involved because you know that you can come back to it later and apply the necessary tweaks to make it better.

6. Start even before you are ready

One of the best ways to not even experience analysis paralysis is to take action before you feel that you are ready. This might sound counterproductive, but it is actually genius. Take for instance Sir Richard Branson, founder and CEO of the Virgin group of companies.

Branson went into countless business ventures and other activities that it is virtually impossible for him to get absolutely ready before deciding on them all. The truth is that it is very unlikely that he was qualified or prepared to get into any of his ventures. For instance, Branson has no idea how to fly a plane, nor does he know the inner intricacies that actually make them fly, and yet he started his own airline company, Virgin Airways, and it is one of the most successful airlines in the world today.

It can be scary just jumping into things without detailed planning, and you are bound to feel uncertainty, as if you believe you are very unprepared and at some degree unqualified. However, the thing is that what you have and what you are right now is enough. Regardless of what you want to do (start your own business, go on a new diet, go back to school, or anything else), you can be sure that the things you know at present is enough for you to get started.

You might feel the strong urge to collect and analyze even more information as a way to somehow overcome your fear of the uncertain that comes when going after big goals. Although there is nothing wrong about planning, but if you feel as if you are stuck in the planning stage, maybe it is about time that you just grit your teeth and take the plunge. So, start even when you feel that you are ready, you will surely figure things out along the way.

7. Believe that your decision is the right one

Overthinkers believe that the best decision is out there, they just need to search a little harder every time. However, the truth is that the choices that are already laid out in front of you has an equal chance of being the best. Anyway, you may not even know which is the best choice.

Many people tend to forget that coming up with a decision is just the first step of the process. The next time you are planning on making a decision, one that is particularly hard to undo the consequences of, it is understandable that you feel like you are on a collision course to failure, and the reason for it is that you are anxious of making the wrong choice and you also have a feeling that the "best" choice is still out there for you to find.

The fact is, making the "best" choice does not always guarantee success, and making a less than desirable choice is also not a sure sign of failure. Whatever choice you make does not matter, what matters is what you do after making a choice. It is often your confidence and commitment to your choice that determines whether the choice you make is "right".

Whenever you are faced with a difficult decision, ask yourself "of all the choices that I have, which one am I more motivated to make a success?". Instead of being caught up in a web of analysis paralysis, use your time and energy to make a solid plan to make your choice into the "best" one.

CONCLUSION

To people who are not suffering from chronic overthinking, this disorder might not seem all that serious. However, for those who are constantly suffering from overthinking day in and day out, it is like being trapped in your own personal hell. Overthinking is like getting trapped in a very small cage that your own mind fabricated; and that cage gets smaller the longer you stay inside it.

Since you have made it to this point of the book, you are now armed with the one thing that you need to get better, and that is knowledge. You now know how to completely eradicate overthinking, or at least minimize its effect on your life. You also now know how to snap yourself out of your funk if ever your mind starts to spiral out of control.

Mindfulness, again, is not a cure-all, however, it does help you manage your overthinking habit. You now know how to identify when you are about to fall into the endless pit of despair made by your overthinking mind, and you also know how to drag yourself out of your funk.

Thank you again for reading this ebook, I hope that this was able to help you manage your overthinking mind before things get even worse.